`D1518242`

Other Books by Norman Finkelstein

Poetry

The Objects In Your Life

Restless Messengers

Track

Columns: Track, Volume 2

Powers: Track, Volume 3

Passing Over

Scribe

Literary Criticism

The Utopian Moment In Contemporary American Poetry

*The Ritual of New Creation: Jewish Tradition and
Contemporary Literature*

*Not One of Them In Place: Modern Poetry and
Jewish American Identity*

Lyrical Interference: Essays On Poetics

*On Mount Vision: Forms of the Sacred In Contemporary
American Poetry*

SCRIBE

by
Norman Finkelstein

DOS MADRES
2009

811
F499s

Dos Madres Press Inc.
P.O. Box 294, Loveland, Ohio 45140
http://www.dosmadres.com
editor@dosmadres.com

Dos Madres is dedicated to the belief that the small press is essential to the vitality of contemporary literature as a carrier of the new voice, as well as the older, sometimes forgotten voices of the past. And in an ever more virtual world, to the creation of fine books pleasing to the eye and hand.

Dos Madres is named in honor of Vera Murphy and Libbie Hughes, the "Dos Madres" whose contributions have made this press possible.

Executive Editor: Robert J. Murphy

Book design & Illustration by Elizabeth Murphy
(www.IllusionStudios.net)

Typeset in
Adobe Garamond Pro & Metal Lord

Library of Congress Control Number: 2009932539

Dos Madres Press, Inc, an Ohio Not is Profit Corporation and a 501(c)(3) qualified public charity.
Contributions are tax deductible.

Acknowledgments

Grateful acknowledgment is made to the editors of the following publications and web sites, where some of the poems in this volume appeared for the first time:

Apex of the M: "Collage."

Cincinnati Review: from *An Assembly* ("Sitting Wall," "Pedestrian Street," "Arcades").

Colorado Review: "At the Threshold"; "For Count Zero"; "Western World."

Cultural Society (www.culturalsociety.net): from *An Assembly* ("Main Gateways," "Entrance Transition," "Tapestry of Light and Dark," "Short Passages"); "Part of Me Belongs Forever to the Fire."

Hambone: "Drones and Chants." Reprinted in *The Best American Poetry 2002,* ed. Robert Creeley (Scribners, 2002).

Notre Dame Review: "Scribe."

Salmagundi: "Like Dates and Almonds, Purple Cloth and Pearls."

Smartish Pace: from *An Assembly* ("Sleeping to the East," " Marriage Bed," and "Couple's Realm"); "Desert."

      Section I of *An Assembly* was published as a Dos Madres Press chapbook under the title *An Assembly.* Special thanks to Robert & Elizabeth Murphy for their love and support.

      An Assembly is based on *A Pattern Language,* by Christopher Alexander and his associates. The poems in my sequence take their titles from one or more of the architectural or design patterns in this book, and all passages within quotation marks in the poems are from the corresponding patterns. My sincere thanks to Christopher Alexander for permission to quote from his work.

Publication of this book was made possible in part through the support of Xavier University.

Illustration

Cover Artwork (c) Copyright 2009, John Bruno Hare. Used by permission. Visit www.sacred-texts.com

Photo of the author by Josephine Hart

TABLE of CONTENTS

Drones and Chants

Collages

An Assembly

IV

DRONES and CHANTS

LIKE DATES AND ALMONDS,
PURPLE CLOTH & PEARLS

in memory of Robert Rethy

We entered by the middle gate
because the first gate frightened us
with the ox and the pit, the destruction and the fire.
We were old men and we were children
old men disguised as children
long ago and yesterday and the day after tomorrow.

We dreamed of it and spoke of it
dreamed that we spoke of it
spoke of it and wrote of it
upon parchments of deerskin.
With the meat we fed the orphans
and on the skins wrote the five books
and took the books to the city
where there were no teachers
and taught five children the five books
and six children the six orders
and told them: We shall return
but in the meantime let each of you
teach his book and his order to all the others.

It was like that and like nothing else
like nothing else in the city
and like nothing in that generation.
It was nothing like nostalgia
though it was said to be all nostalgia
like a word twisted into a ring
and like a ring lost in a deep pool
and like a ring found in the belly of a fish
that spoke so it might return to the sea.

It was built by the water so as to wait there.
The word came from across the water
the word flowed into other words
the water poured down and we stood there naked
looking out to a horizon that stretched across the world.
We wanted to go back and would have
had it not been for all the errors
in the memories and in the recording of the memories
and in the recording of the recording
in the city of cities across the water.

We wanted it to go on and it did go on
though it stopped and it turned and so turned up
elsewhere wherever between here and the river
that threw up stones for six days out of seven.
We could not rest though we longed for rest
we had returned though we did not think to return
we looked and we saw ourselves under the canopy of the horizon
and it was as we had been taught though we could no longer
    remember.

SCRIBE

You enter the city with harps and with flutes,
with drums and with baskets
of grapes and pomegranates.
You enter the city of blue ash and blue spruce,
that terraced city rumored of the spirit.

You come there as would a fire,
but neither you nor anything you touch is burned.
There is no sign upon you,
but there are signs upon the doorposts,
amulets of silver shaped like a hand
with letters upon the palm and fingers.

You wander into the little streets
unguarded by leopards or the statues of leopards,
where love is brought to you like an offering
stolen from the altar of a civic deity
who blesses the family with contentment.

You may say you have failed your calling,
that your riches and your debts have taken you this far
and will take you farther, you who have traded
upon yourself and upon the idols that you broke and
    reassembled.

You have written a history of renunciation
and a genealogy of indulgence,
mistaking pleasure for experience
and experience for wisdom.
You have raised your voice against the sufficiency of silence,
and answered by silence you were silenced,
but never with sufficient severity
and never without sufficient hope.

You have heeded the word of the outside god
and you have heeded the word of no god at all,
like a prophet turned archaeologist,
a scribe turned into a scribe.

MY FATHER DINES WITH THE CAPTAIN

Lift up your head from your labors
and hands, cease from your work.
My father dines with the Captain tonight;
nothing in memory or in the fields of sight
can be as strange or as fair.

                                    You on the ship
in those tropical seas, what do you know
of their conversation? Do not break the spell
too soon. My father speaks and the Captain,
grey in his beard but with the vigor of age,
replies. Do not break the spell.
The moon is rising over tropical seas;
my father leaves the cabin, limping to the rail.
You on the ship, take heed:
do not listen but do not forget. Nothing in memory
or on the ocean of sight can be as strange.

The Captain keeps his log. My father writes
a few words in a journal. My father broke
the spell, sailing the warm, the moon-loved sea
and limping upon the land. The Captain smiles.
What does he know? His log is an ocean,
full of long voyages, and my father is but one man
with whom he dines. You on the ship,
passengers and crew, what lights have you seen
descend upon the coasts, what northern lights
as you head out of summer at the Captain's command?

He turns the wheel. Is it haze
around the moon or a wheel in a wheel
that my father sees? He leans against the rail,
looking up, looking out. It can go on,
sing the beasts below in the sea. It can go on,
sing the passengers and the crew together,
dreaming of romance as they cross the line.

They do not want the spell to be broken.
They do not want to sail out of summer seas,
but my father sees the light on the horizon
and the Captain turns the wheel. His hands
return to their labors and my father
limps upon the land.

THE HEDGE

One after another
I raised them up
as if the hedge around the book
were a ring around the moon

One after another
I sent them out
and none came back
in all the time after

And if I were to meet one on the way
he would be happy to remind me
of the book and of the saying
over the book

that I had nearly forgotten
so long ago
that I thought I had heard it elsewhere
though I had said it myself

I mean I had said it all
I mean I had said nothing
I mean he had forgotten nothing
while I had forgotten it all

as if the hedge
were a ring around the moon
and the moon were to come down
in a forgetful embrace

Love of the moment
love between the spheres
erasing the memory
of all that had been said

until love itself
became a memory
recalled in the book
and the saying over the book

that is the hedge
spoken in moonlight
shining on the way
like a silver kiss

VALENTINE

And if his heart were a lute
on which she could play

And if her hair were the strings
of a harp that was his heart

And if he were bound down
by the cords of her hair

And if her red hair
were the cords of his heart

And if the chords resound
and echo in the chamber

The empty chamber
after all is past

The end is silence
but for the stirring of her heart

The breath from her lips
at the open chamber

And if love broke its head
and she held it in her hands

Red hands red chamber
the last and the first

And if the chords passed
beyond the bounds of utterance

To become utterance

So that he said it was day
and that love was alive

Living in the chamber
of her red red heart

THE RELEASE

Over the border you look with longing
until one day there is only longing
waiting to be fulfilled.

You drive and drive in love's dominion,
hardly thinking you will meet with danger
forgotten and yet foretold.

There are static streams in a fluid world,
measured lines where the meadows curl
in upon themselves like prayer.

There is weather, and the weather threatens;
there are figures, and the figures beckon
to a place of perfect rest.

The lovers rise up from the leaves around you
and their kisses are the sound of leaves around you
and all their kisses are leaves.

LAMP

Light love
falls upward
falls over
us as we
lie together

Love's sight
rises downward
each particle
kisses utter
each syllable

Sight's shade
dims toward
reaching above
hand's darkness
speaking love

THE PSYCHE ADRIFT

thinking of Henry Weinfield's Mallarmé

The psyche adrift
In love's domain

Cries to the Master
Standing apart:

Where is the heart
That once was the center?

When will you enter
The widening rift?

And what refrain
Must I sing and sing

To lure your word
From vacant space

That love might record
And never erase?

Peace, came the answer,
Fold your wings.

PART OF ME BELONGS FOREVER TO THE FIRE

Part of me belongs forever to the fire
For I am a spark of the flame thereof.
Beyond the business of the world, part of me is burning
And burned there fiercely before I was born.
Fatherless and motherless, the orphaned spark
Finally fell from an infinite height
Until finally finite, it passed into the world,
Was held and named and knew itself to be.

Part of me is a part forever of the world
And part of me stands apart continually burning.
What would you touch if you would touch my heart?
In its vacancy it is naught but stone and air,
Air compounded, pounded upon a stone,
Until a spark ignites in that sealed space,
Until a spark unites with the fire beyond,
More distant than any body can bear.

Therefore I ask you: what is love
If out of stone and air and unbearable distance
This spark has been flung far from the fire?
Souls shrivel in the flame that I am,
Bodies and souls in a rain of ashes,
Bodies and souls in the rain of disaster,
So that long after, in the business of the world,
One longs to burn and burn in the flame.

FOR COUNT ZERO

A machine in a dome making boxes
A machine in a novel making boxes
A novel machine making boxes

He said there is loneliness and loneliness
It said it was never sad
She said there are sadnesses and sadnesses

It said once I was not
It said once without duration I was everything
It said the bright time broke

It said these things you treasure are shells
She said you are someone else's collage
Was it the mad daughter?

She watched the objects float by
Vial of perfume armless doll silk cravat black fountain pen
To be sorted by the poet

He thought he was outside the novel
He was mistaken and then
He knew he was mistaken

He wanted the machine to place him in a box
Like the leather from her jacket
Vain, the scattered fragments of myself, like children

And the boy didn't like it
Because he knew too much about it
But then again he might not

A fictitious future
Posing as a real future
Becoming the real future

All this is quotation
Even if it is not all quotation
The sadness the dance the song

My songs are of time and distance
The sadness is in you
Watch my arms

WESTERN WORLD

after Idoru

There was one whose face was a narrative
There was one whose life was a corporation
There was one made entirely of light

There was rain made entirely of light
Even at night while the buildings grew
Rising out of the robotic mist

Mist moving like phlogiston
Celebrity moving like phlogiston
Alchemical marriage of the stars

And he fell into her eyes
Into dreams of snow on the steppes
And her eyes falling away

Or celebrity as presentation
The Etruscan as centipede
Waving his little hands

At Klaus and the Rooster
Ghosts among the cubicles
Stolen and stolen again

Their dry insect voices
Scratchy sounds like laughter
Endlessly remixed

Like a children's story
Because the girl gets home safe
And the ogre is happy

Happy among the corporations
Happy among the narratives
Telling of crime and fame

DRONES AND CHANTS

in memory of Armand Schwerner

All night long they turned the wheels,
picked up the sound and passed it on

All night long we listened to the music,
all night there was thunder among the hills

All night and day the words were spoken,
each word inscribed and traced to its origin

All night and day the words were sung,
picked up, inscribed, and passed along

So as forever to be forgotten,
rising and breaking against the air

The sound floated above the valley
like mist gathering over deep pools

The mist rose above the trees in the valley,
blooming into emblems of silence

Emblems of mist and emblems of trees,
cast forever into the pools of night

The instruments were gathered up from the pools
and all night long they turned the wheels

COLLAGES

COLLAGE
in memory of Helen Adam

*   *   *

Carnival at the edge of town

Woman in a turban with a jewel
telling fortunes

Lady in suede gloves goes by
three greyhounds at her heel

Once again the heart is transfixed.

*   *   *

Crow Castle
November, 19__

Dear J,

    I have no one but myself to blame for this predicament. When the affair exploded, Crow Castle proved my only choice. You can well imagine what it was like getting here. Suffice it to say that they did not treat me gently. But all that ended once I arrived. Indeed, a great deal ended, or rather, changed so dramatically it seemed to have ended. Everything we had come to associate with "the other side" fell away. From all outward appearance, life here proceeds normally. Except for certain duties which I first performed with reluctance, but now find quite tolerable, I am left alone. There are a few others here, so we have been able to compare notes, as it were. No two histories are really similar, but certain common themes do emerge.

    You may recall that, before I was compelled to leave, we discussed the role of the will in the various arts we practiced. Both of us were attached (rather sentimentally) to a notion favored by our contemporaries; that is, it is best to relinquish one's will in seeking to achieve transformation. Under the proper conditions, the new, desired form could appear instantaneously and with no apparent effort on the practitioner's part; his task having lay instead only in the arrangement of those conditions. Only there, we allowed, did the will come into play, and just to set the scene and perhaps maintain a certain flexibility or efficiency of the instruments. Sooner or later (and how much patience was always demanded!), such powers as may arrive or may already inhabit the artist's world would set the process in motion, and in that most pleasurable, most wrenching moment of achievement, the form would stand forth.

I know now from sad experience that we had forgotten one crucial element—not lack of craft, not human frailty, not even chance, but something I must call, however portentously, the abyss. When we shut our eyes, it may appear that we have relinquished our will, but we are only gathering ourselves before we leap. And whether we land upon the other side or plummet downward, it is "in the shooting of the gulf," as one of our order once put it, that transformation takes place.

I offer these observations despite the feeling that, for me at least, such matters are now beside the point. Years seem to pass between the writing of one sentence and another, between the thinking of two consecutive thoughts. What is found in the passage between? It is there, I suppose, that the "magic" is to be found, if it is to be found anywhere at all. Crow Castle itself may well be such a passage, despite the sense that I may be here forever. The two notions are by no means mutually exclusive: I have taken up residence in a place that is always elsewhere.

So it seems that you should not expect my return any time soon. I'll try to get word to you again after the spring thaw. Please send my regards to the crowd at the Cafe Luna. Is Tony still calling himself Antoine since the place changed hands? And of course, remember me to Suzanne.

As ever,

R.

PS Looking out from the east tower, I can see that the troops
are on the move again.

*   *   *

Man-headed dog
Dog-headed man

White cat, gold cat
Moth with eyes upon its wings

Eyes behind the screen
At the foot of the bed

Naked they grapple
And in the skies above

This house is made strange by love.

*   *   *

And by a waterfall

                     a furious angel

And in the chamber

                     a rat and a goose

And in the chamber

                     a severed hand

And in the chamber of the skull

                     no rest, no rest.

*   *   *

In the sequence of invention
you come to a place

The turns in the maze
that lead to empty laughter

One turn beyond the mirror
two beyond the sea

And if you love her you will know
you will know you love her.

* * *

My father was a minister
and my mother was the girl
he had found on the moors

My father had a walking stick
with the head of a dog

My father had a walking stick
that walked by itself

My father's dog
walked by mother's side

Walked and walked
when she was lost on the moors

My father's mother
found the moors
guarded by dogs

With eyes big as saucers
and voices of brass

Lie down lie down
say the voices of brass

Lie down say the voices
of silk and brass

In mother's parlor
in father's parlor
in mother's parlor

No longer to walk
like a dog by my side.

*   *   *

The magic rises
from love in despair

Desire returning
as a vengeful ghost

The ghost of old Egypt
howling across the Nile

Incarnated in an oak tree
in the center of the field

Incarnated in the empty
center of the maze

The name of the maze is Troy Town
or Troynovant, where love lived and died

Or the Elfin Pedlar
where love lived and died

The humming top and the dove
and the death of love.

*   *   *

have tried to convey the intrusiveness of these voices through the use of italics, but I am not altogether satisfied with the result. And there seems to be nothing I can do to give the reader the sense of simultaneity which the visual artist can achieve, but which the writer, working through time rather than space, cannot reproduce in anywhere near a convincing fashion. The inevitable linearity of even the most disjunctive series of texts

* * *

This is the withdrawal of the frame

This is the loss of the context

This is where

And this is where

A cat encrypted in a wall or on a wall

An invisible dwarf beating us all at chess

References to cats and chess

I could make this rhyme but I have been emptied
    of desire

Still a ballad.

* * *

As a girl, a prodigy
at death, a ward of the state

How many files opened
how many miles travelled

How many sisters loved and lost
how many in the counting rhyme

One two three
four five six

Seven
and six different men

And a unicorn.

*   *   *

AT THE THRESHOLD

for Robert Murphy

At the entrance
To the godhouse
Above the Janus door

On the heart's entablature
Frieze
Of our remaking

In my right hand
The flower
Of my consolations

In my left
A fountain of petals
Out of a cane of thorns.

* * *

No
Consolation

As if we
Too had drunk
At the star-well

As if we
Were with him on
The way to language

Yellow stars
In a black forest.

* * *

But your
Omphalos house
Holds true

Promise of rest
A threshold
To myth

Hedgehog
Wolfhound
A set table

Who would not
Cross
Over?

* * *

To what
Occasion can we
Rise

Toward what
Stars what
Fire

What have
You you
Myth

Builder house
Raiser
Kin

To what species
What family
Lost

Brother to my
Orphaned my
Widowed

Insufferable but
Still articulate
Soul?

*   *   *

Take everything
From life but
Give nothing
To biography

Who
Speaks who
Has the right to speak
For whom?

You enact
The deed of presence
You pass
Into manifestation

You
Are authorized
You
Remain unknown

Scholium:
"Poems create poets."

*   *   *

And you you
Third you
Other you
I entered you

Who are always
Entering

Whom I could never
Keep out

My star my
Red star
Always rising
Above me.

*   *   *

With this I
Call you all
Together

With this I
Charm you al-
Though when I

Speak I mis-
Speak I lose
What binds us

One to ten-
Uous
One

Make me
Your lyre
Make me

Tell you all
A story
Bord-

Ering
on
Truth.

    * * *

       (Rosh Hashanah)

Sorrow
Division

There is
No measure

There is
No judge

But Isaac is released

And Samuel is brought to speech.

    * * *

Threshold of
Love when she
Bade me enter

Threshold of
Friendship where
I was restored

Threshold beyond
Threshold that is
The work

Made strange
But not made
Strange enough

Made to resemble
A god
With two faces

One looking toward
The west and one
Looking toward syntax

One speaking
To a god and one
Really speaking

On the threshold of
The threshold where
We find a name

Where we find
The line moving
Away from

Any sense
Any god
Any name.

* * *

My lost one
My vagrant star
My bird

With two nests.

     *   *   *

DESERT

for John B. Hare

The pronomial outcry, as if uttered in ecstasy,
Is turned to syntax.
                    —*Harvey Shapiro*

The world cried out above the mountain.
                    —*George Oppen*

1.

Clouded sky filled with letters,
Hebrew letters stretching
to the horizon, pale
stripe of blue;

Inscribed desert floor
reaching to the base
of the many-peaked mountain,
striated tans and browns;

Fire as tall as the
mountain, pure red,
more spirit than fire,
shadow on sand.

2.

No one climbing these peaks;
no one guided by
this pillar of flame. No one
crossing these sands; no one
seeking meaning in this sky.

3.

Shadow and flame and peaks like knives:
the letters rearrange themselves again
and again. Not meaning but the promise
of meaning; not events in time
but time to hold all events.

4.

And to have come a long way,
always thinking about the voices,
the promises, reiterations, charges,
and declarations. The stories the voices
told, and the stories told about the voices.

5.

Called back, returned, and so went forth
again. From the edge of the abyss, "the
deep places of the imagination," retrieved,
rescued, redeemed. Fronted, confronted,
conspired, conspired against, usurped
stolen, sacrificed. Bidden, forbidden.
Dreamed, prophecied, spoke to, with,
against. Visited, was visited, was visited
upon. Throned. Dethroned. Written
upon the sky and upon the ground.

6.

Neither upon the sky nor upon the ground

Neither in the desert nor at the mountain

Neither in the heights nor in the depths

Neither present nor absent

Neither known nor unknown

Neither strange nor familiar

Neither whole nor in fragments

Neither revealed nor hidden

Neither sacred nor profane

Neither spoken nor silent.

7.

And you, once
the image fades,
the screen goes
blank, do you still
hover above the whole
picture, beyond the
numbers that program,
the letters that inscribe,
the voice that speaks
this desert world?

COLLAGE IV

* * *

Lady Isabel sits a-sewing
            [*Fine flowers in the valley*]
When she heard the Elf Knight's horn a-blowing
            [*As the roses blow*]

The free movement of tense
present to past
indicates
an eternal present
or eternal past

or so it would seem

* * *

Indicates an eternal desire
to nurse an elf child
a deadly child
or deadly lover
deadly father
lost or slain

Would I had that horn a-blowing
            [*Fine flowers in the valley*]
And yon Elf Knight for to sleep in my bosom
            [*As the roses blow*]

                              *   *   *

Unvoiced chorus
Unvoiced lines
Missing lines

Unsung

Scarcely had she these words spoken
                    [*Fine flowers in the valley*]
When in at the window the Elf Knight's broken
                    [*As the roses blow*]

                              *   *   *

At some point you must
release the song
forget the song
as Isabel
forgot her desire

                    —exchanged—

for deeper love

                              *   *   *

                    sword belt

                                        dagger

* * *

And like a ship the heart
sails out to sea
(another song
scarcely remembered)

       (here is the fiddle
       here the drum)

loaded deep
but not as deep
as the love I miss

             Come and nurse an elf child
             Down beneath the sea

* * *

The water is wide
We cannot get o'er
And neither have
I wings to fly

          But I have a pretty boatman
          Ferryman
          Ferryman

This is the water
I would cross to you

* * *

And at some point the voice
may intervene

And at some point a voice
may carry you back

Carry you across
with wings and sails

* * *

Neither wings nor sails
neither sword belt nor dagger

Then lie you here a husband to them all
                    [*As the roses blow*]

* * *

AN ASSEMBLY

"let the site tell you its secrets"

I

SLEEPING TO THE EAST

so that "The sun
        warms you,
                increases the light,
                        gently nudges you to wake up"

so that you can speak to the sun
speak of the day
with someone beside you

The poem like a room
providing morning light
like a window through which
falls light from the east
upon a bed that provides
a view of the light, fruit trees, gardens,
and the lawn beyond
or courtyard, terrace,
somewhere to walk

        The poem like the day beginning
        "at the moment which serves you best
        —that is, just after a dream."

MARRIAGE BED

on which such light as there is
mornings
may fall
"the center of a couple's life together:
the place where they lie together,
      talk,
           make love,
                sleep,
                    sleep late,
take care of each other during illness"

in such light as is there

"The space around the bed
is shaped around the bed
      . . . slightly enclosed, with a low ceiling or canopy
      . . . perhaps a tiny room built around the bed
      with many windows"

"Quite honestly, we are not certain whether or not this pat-
tern makes sense. On the one hand, it does: it is a beautiful
idea; idyllic almost. Yet, face to face with cold hard fact and
with the dissolution and struggles in the marriages around
us, it seems hard to hope that it could ever be quite real.
We have decided to leave it in, just because it is a beautiful
idea"

The poem as an idea of rest entwined
around two bodies resting entwined
around all their time together
Always one wants to rest
in the other, one wants a space
that is the other resting at anchor
One said there isn't an anchor
in the drift of the world, "dissolution

and struggles," and indeed one wakes
in the midst of a dream, not in light
but in enduring darkness
One said the bed was a great distance
between them, and we took it, rightly,
for a bad sign

But the dawn comes
and love may return, out of intimacy
love may return, secure a place
again for itself in the poem

"unlikely that the bed can come
to have the right feeling until a couple
has weathered some hard times together

and there is some depth to their experience."

COUPLE'S REALM

"that is, a world
in which the intimacy of the man and woman,
their joys and sorrows
can be shared and lived through"

not behind closed doors
but removed enough in space and mind
that the binding power
which first defined them
may continue to thrive

"distinct from the common areas
and all the children's rooms"

And when you go and when you return
by day or by night
love's exits and entrances
can be hard to bear
In time we understand
it is a drama and therefore
needs a stage on which to unfold
Actors and audience, we
let events pass or else force them
to crisis, come what may
If there were "a sitting room,
a place for privacy, a place for projects";
if the bed were "tucked away
into an alcove with its own window"

Such is love's
utopian vista
and real space

which I cannot abandon

"Give this place a quick path
to the children's rooms, but,
at all costs,
make it a distinctly separate realm."

CHILDREN'S REALM

"almost like a wide swath
inside the house,
muddy, toys strewn along the way,
touching those family rooms
which children need"

so that I wonder
how well we managed
to give them a world

> The second floor
> with its play space
> and bedrooms
> Summoned upstairs,
> we were guests,
> never knowing who
> or what would greet us

Now they occupy
the common areas,
make them their own,
retreat only rarely
into bedrooms for the solitude
we always seem to crave

This
was to be a sort of farewell,
whatever other frenzies
may visit us. Shall we
let go of their childhood
and still cling to our own?
What was it led me
back to that realm
except the discovery
of my own needs

otherwise inexpressible
except through a language
of terror and enchantment?

"If there is an adequate children's world,
in the manner described in this pattern,
then both the adults and children
can co-exist, each without dominating the other"

I want it so within myself
and within those I love—
a continuum of spaces
where the child at play
may pass by or enter
that place common to all
of my being

                    Nor can it be
too far from that grown-up world
also of bodies and minds

of storms and of the peace after storms

the child and adult facing each other
          across a space that is all
                    terror and enchantment.

CHILDREN'S HOME

in memory of Robert Duncan

Thinking now
that his work has always been
a safe haven for me,

> I return to the pattern book and find
> "a place where children can be safe
> and well looked after"

For I go into the work
as a child, seeking
"a second family"
"large rambling house or workplace"
"with a public path passing across the site"

To go between worlds
the strange hermeneutic
passage between adult and child

So that the longing for magic
is the longing for comfort
questing powers
effecting awaited return

> And that I was taught there!
> delighted that the work
> was actually play
> and that the teacher
> was a mage who also
> had come home

> "In effect, it is a real home of some people;
> it does not close down at night"

But is there
whenever I need
that care

Wonder of the youth
heading toward manhood
wonder that so much
could be saved

To sit on a low wall
talking to passers-by
to visit those rooms and open spaces
knowing there is a common
place at the heart

to which I return.

ADVENTURE PLAYGROUND

or go out to a place
full of "all kinds of junk"

>   "—nets, boxes, barrels,
>   trees, ropes, simple tools,
>   frames, grass, and water—"

wrestling with a picture of the world

Here the play
is wilder, the poem
gets built out of anything

>   Caves and huts
>   gradually accreting
>   or attracting names
>   which become increasingly communal
>   as the season moves along

>   Then to tear it all down
>   make a bonfire
>   have a dance and cart
>   the rest off to old folks
>   to light their hearths

Where am I
that I could even dream of such things?
I would have the work
hold to a kind of modesty
however flamboyant it may appear
With uncanny joy I found myself
in a place rigged out of cardboard,
scraps of wood and twine,
knowing it could collapse
with the slightest gesture

Call this one
A Parable of Anarchy
assembled
in another world.

CHILDREN IN THE CITY

and beyond
a network of safe paths
the city as school or playground
changing at a whim

an open city
with great swatches of common land,
markets, promenades, public squares, cafes,
ribbons of industry and scattered work,
bike paths, green streets, local
town halls and services,
still water, birth places,
graves and sacred sites

       and to deal with this
       vagueness and unboundedness
       as the poem like the
       "adventurous young"
       goes forth to teach
       to learn and play

Ruptures
appear in the text
constitute
the house of the life being lived
In town "There is a small
but ominous danger . . ."

       Yet "the path goes past
       and through interesting parts
       of the city;
       and it is relatively safe"

That it enters the contours
of the larger patterns;
accommodates smaller needs
and minor desires along
its sinuous way

"down pedestrian streets,
through workshops, assembly plants,
print houses, bakeries,
all the interesting
'invisible' life of a town"

Perhaps
(he could write in the next letter)
we must take the risk
The poem resists closure
courts formlessness for the sake of growth
as this unlikely
private soul
risks civic utterance

"Line the children's path with windows,
especially from rooms that are in frequent use,
so that the eyes upon the street
make it safe for the children."

BEER HALL

"Where can people sing, and drink,
            and shout and drink,
            and let go of their sorrows?"

One sits down
next to another
who invites a third

                    and they drink

One speaks to another
of where he has been
what he has seen

                    and they drink

One wonders
how he has come
to be here
"the bar, the dance floor,
a fire, darts"
a crowded place
"with beer and wine,
music"

                    so he drinks

                    caught
                    in a spell of forgetfulness
                    a communal forgetting
                    set to music

                    heard across the hall

Looking into the fire
thinking of the shapes
one loses track
of where he has been
what he has seen

        dancing clumsily
        with strangers
        who are suddenly friends.

DANCING IN THE STREET

But where the lanterns shine
in an open square
and the music draws you
along the promenade

        you may find it

"The embarrassment
and the alienation
are recent developments,
blocking a more basic need
And as we get in
touch with these needs

            things start to happen"

            The life of the city
            may be only the life
            of the mind   the street
            could kill you   the street
            could bring you back to life
            but only if
            "People remember how to dance;
            everyone takes up an instrument;
            many hundreds form little bands."

PROMENADE

"People come to see people
and to be seen"
"to walk up and down,
to meet their friends,
to stare at strangers,
and to let strangers stare at them"

> Stare and stare
> fill the eyes
> with the sight of others
> who are ourselves
> acting ourselves

"These places have always been
like street theaters:

> "This destination may
> be real, like a coke shop
> or cafe, or it may
> be partly imaginary"

> What
> are you looking for in this
> ordered swirl,
> current of "people
> with a shared way of life"
> which is yours though you
> think of yourself apart
> seeking traces
> of what is always here

"ice cream parlors,
coke shops, churches,
public gardens, movie houses,
bars, volleyball courts"

Walking along at rest
with yourself and others.

QUIET BACKS

Hurried along . . .

Went through . . .

Came out behind . . .

> "a long ribbon
> of quiet alleyways
> which converge on the local
> pools and streams
> and the local greens"

> So that the buildings,
> the sites of noisy life,
> shield us,
> offer a temporary
> respite

> > Couples, small groups, solitary
> > walkers,
> > thoughtful souls
> > seated beneath trees
> > "where the mood is slow
> > and reflective"

And I know

why you have come here

I know

how long you've been gone

how brief will be your stay

sound of bees
among the columbines
sound of water
falling over the wall falling from
pool to pool.

GRAVE SITES

. . . Nearby, just off the path, we came upon a little grave site, roughly triangular in shape, enclosed by a low stone wall and shaded by a willow. The gate was open; we entered and stood about, or sat upon an iron bench which faced the graves—some two or three of them, it being difficult to determine the precise number. There had been some settling; the stones had tilted, and one had actually cracked in half; though on closer examination, the graves seemed of no great age. The inscriptions on the stones were indecipherable: among our group, some recognized the alphabet but did not know the language, while others had never seen such writing before. Our guide was at a loss to explain the site; he knew no stories connected with it, nor had any previous sightseers enquired of him about it. It was, however, a pleasant spot in its own melancholy way; and certain members of our party remained there for some time, in quiet reflection or simply enjoying the cool breeze.

II

As I said to the Pattern Master:

Why is it I must return
to this eternal school of forms?
What have I still to learn
about building a life in time?
Will I never cease to yearn
to hear the sentences pronounced?
What is it I must discern
before I see the whole in the part?

Since the language is in truth a network,
there is no sequence which perfectly captures it.

MAIN GATEWAYS

Where the path crosses the boundary
into an important precinct—
"made more sharp, more
vivid, more alive"

places of industry or craft
places of law and judgment
of civic life
dwelling places
of distinct groups, subcultures
that yet reach out
to the general populace

    "It will be there,
        it will be felt,
                only if the crossing is marked"

                "a literal gate, a bridge,
                a passage between narrowly
                separated buildings, an avenue
                of trees, a gateway
                through a building"

                At the boundary
                of some neighborhood
                or building complex
                "the crucial feeling
                which this solid thing
                must create
                is the feeling of transition"

        Open
        these great gateways
        that have always
        been open

Mark every boundary
every place between

I say open the gates
that they may stand
open I say open
the gates.

ENTRANCE TRANSITION

And there are other boundaries
other crossings
other transitions
on a more intimate scale
"a more intimate spirit
appropriate to a house"

                                    Pass now
                                    by way of an "entry court"
                                    "bend in the path"
                                    "a long sheltered gallery
                                    from which there is a view

                                    into the distance"

                    Come in
                    to my house my
                    life   I have come
                    this far into this
                    seclusion I would
                    offer to you too

                    I would lay it out
                    point it out starting
                    here in the courtyard
                    this bit of garden
                    where you may find
                    me leading you or
                    lingering, waiting
                    for others

the gate, the path
            to some place that is ours, open
                        to everyone but not everyone's

some place that holds
        to a kind of courtesy
                    and welcome.

TAPESTRY OF LIGHT AND DARK

Flood the entrances
and paths with light
but reserve some
spots for shadow

We linger
in pools of light
but would steal away
upon occasion
into the adjacent darkness

                    "Much loved and much used
                    places": "window seats,
                    verandas, fireside
                    corners, trellised arbors"

                    The shadows flicker
                    among the varied
                    sources of light

                    to which we are drawn

And in this tapestry
of our homes, our
lives, our ideal that
has been stolen from us
that we have stolen from ourselves
and that I so
wish to return—

Look! Bronk
said it was only
the light, but Duncan
knew the uneven
was unbounded though
the hearth was at the center

I recall the great stove
with the coal room behind
the kitchen table by the window
looking out toward the garden
the sun room where the vines
curled up through the floor boards

                and all of this is gone
                it is gone
                into a world of light

My companions
        my lost ones
                and those to whom
                        I would still cling

        If this tapestry is life lived
        light alternating
        with great darkness I
        call upon you all
        never to abandon it

We hold to the house
        we wander in error
                from place to place for

"there is good reason to believe
that people need
a rich variety of settings
in their lives"

As we have dwelt there
        as we have moved
                through light and dark.

SHORT PASSAGES

Generosity of movement   Generosity of light

                    In the Circulation Realm
                    to which each building
                    contributes, a nested
                    system of realms
                    so ordered and named

                    In every building
                    office or dwelling place
                    public or private

                    We come, going
                    from here to there

                    through light, passing
                    bookcases, windows,
                    benches built
                    into the wall where
                    one may pause
                    in the midst of things

What would make
this passage short,
animated, alive

to where we are going
from where we have come?

                    A corridor
                    "generous in shape"
                    devoted to our needs
                    and loved therefore
                    as much as any room.

HALF-HIDDEN GARDEN/
GARDEN GROWING WILD/
GARDEN WALL

There is a place
off to the side
of the house
a place where
"mosses and grasses
will grow between
paving stones"—a place
with "some kind of tenuous
connection to the street
and entrance"—a place
just intimate enough,
private enough, "yet
open enough through

        paths, gates, arcades, trellises"

        There is a place free
        to grow, that need not
        "be tended obsessively"
        that can be left alone and
        "will not go to ruin
        in one or two seasons"

        Between "wilderness
        and cultivation"
        I have sought a site,
        sought to plant and build
        and in doing so discover
        uncover
        my heart's desire

When you are here
it may be
I am in that place
and when you are gone
I remain at least
for a time

If the world
is too much with us
or not with us enough

If that balance fails
or if we fail
that balance

I am called upon to seek,
to plant, to build

And oh! how I have always wanted it
"shielded from the sight and sound
of passing traffic" yet "*open*
to the rush of life around it."

SITTING WALL

Soft tile and brick
to build a low wall
righting the "injustice
to the subtlety
of the divisions between the spaces"

Outdoor rambles
from here to there

The snow is gone
but the air still braces

Crocuses
in full bloom

The earth
pools

But here it is dry
—Come
and sit by me

On this low wall
legs swinging
side by side

Barriers that separate
seams that join

Again and again
the wall may run
and we may rest
and talk a bit
exchange

a secret or two

For the boundary
is ambiguous
and seated upon it
spaces open
on either side

(There were ornaments
in the garden
and in the flower beds the stones
spoke to me

PEDESTRIAN STREET

But now I have lost
myself among the people
wanted to lose
myself among the sheltered
streets, the many
entrances, the open
stairs taking me
up and down among
strangers and friends

Strangers become friends
become a bit more
known in the density
of innumerable passages
from the shops and offices
homes of the pedestrians
who may live their lives freely
walking from place to place

I imagine you coming
toward me   Have you
been shopping or merely
strolling about? How good
to see you here now
that you are settling in
looking down from your room
above the square

I recall that the street
led to a little plaza
with a fountain, a café,
toy shop, bookseller,
greengrocer and that curious
store full of fabrics and rugs

I can't return
because it never was
I never even read it
in the pattern book
though it has
brought this forth
it has brought
this forth in the open work
of my days

How much
planning must we do
and how much
can we simply wander
in that street that is a world
and how much
will it cost in the end?

Have you managed?
Have you been
as careful as you can?
Sit here and rest
until I return.)

STREET CAFÉ

They were drinking Wolf's Head, a wine
from somewhere up north
or Bull's Blood,
from somewhere to the east

They were drinking *kaffee mit schlag*
or Campari, something
bitter or something sweet

Bittersweet, it was "a risky place"
but "part of their life-blood"

It was in their blood,
to "be very public"
however relaxed, waiting for
"perhaps the next person . . ."
to walk beneath the awning
out of the bright sun
into softer light.

They were telling stories
while in the story

They were making deals
or making love,
loved dealing
with each other, the tables
close together though one could still feel
comfortably alone.

The newspapers
announced that they were reading
the newspapers

The newspapers
announced that they would all be in
the newspapers

It was public knowledge
however intimate
what they said
when they shook hands
or whispered
in someone's ear.

SMALL PUBLIC SQUARES/
HIERARCHY OF OPEN SPACE/ACTIVITY POCKETS/
SOMETHING ROUGHLY IN THE MIDDLE/
PUBLIC OUTDOOR ROOMS

"shops, stands, benches, displays,
rails, courts, gardens, news racks"

> "small crowds, festivals, bonfires,
> carnivals, speeches, dancing,
> shouting, mourning"

> > "a partly enclosed place,
> > with some roof, columns,
> > without walls, perhaps
> > with a trellis"

> > "a fountain, a tree, a statue,
> > a clocktower with seats,
> > a windmill, a bandstand"

There is a bench outside the shop
across from the café
where the bus stops once an hour
weekdays

You were strolling
        down the path
                toward the fountain

I saw you, I
called to you

["A person's face is just recognizable
at about 70 feet;
and under typical urban noise
conditions, a loud voice
can just barely be heard
across 70 feet."]

And in the garden looking out
into the square, we saw
the children buying ice cream
and comics at the kiosk

Contained, adjacent
to a larger space,
easily negotiated,
traversed by paths
and sight lines

Opening out
from "a garden, terrace,
street, park, public
outdoor room, or courtyard"

Something is happening
something can happen
busy and yet
at a relaxed pace

music

conversation

ACCESS TO WATER/
POOLS AND STREAMS/
STILL WATER

Because "We came from the water;"
because "our bodies are largely water;"
because "we went back to the sea
and lived 10 million years as
sea mammals in the shallow water
along the edge of the ocean"—

you and I sought
the bank of the stream,
walked "lazily along the edge"
just where it flowed
into the pond

There by the shallows
under the willows
dreams seemed
more accessible

                    "a natural gradient,
                    which changes as a person
                    comes up to the edge,
                    and goes on changing as the water
                    is first very shallow,
                    and then gradually gets deeper"

Gradually the "fundamental yearning
for great bodies of water"
becomes harder to satisfy
The water's edge "falls
into private hands"
but "the land immediately
along the water's edge
must be preserved for common use"

Can there be a space
by water partly
secluded but still
on public land

Can there be a place
for us upon the shore
secluded but near
children "free to play
around a pool"

"they can sit at the edge
and have their feet in the water,
or walk along with
the water around their ankles"

In dreams of "ponds and pools"
in dreams that are "reservoirs,
and in brooks and streams"
we seek each other, summon
our selves across
"in an endless local texture
of small pools, ponds, reservoirs,
and streams in every neighborhood"
we have seen our reflections
running and running away

On every occasion
you are touched by water
pause and reflect
upon "its limits and its mystery"

SACRED SITES/HOLY GROUND

Even in exile
even in the book
even of the book

      one approaches

            "a series of nested precincts,
            each one marked by a gateway,
            each one progressively more private,
            and more sacred than the last,
            the innermost a final sanctum

            that can only be reached

                  by passing through

                        all of the outer ones"

And because one's life
is a series of gateways
because one must wait for a
"gradual revelation, passage
through a series of gates"

because back of every mind
centered in every heart
there is "a building or a tree,
or rock or stone"

            "A garden which can be reached only
            by passing through a series of outer gardens

            keeps its secrecy.

A temple which can be reached only
by passing through a sequence of approach courts
is able to be a special thing in a man's heart."

And *your* heart?
What is it but an endless
series of gateways toward
what love or has it
turned monstrous, blocked,
guarded fiercely by archons
as Kafka saw?

Worse yet, it is
"bulldozed, developed, changed
for political and economic reasons,
without regard for these simple
and fundamental emotional matters."

Against which I have only
the line, devoted to, enthralled by
the book. You pilgrims, go
neither to Canterbury nor Mecca.
There is a mountain, there is
a river, follow from one stanza
to the next.

Wait here.

Wait here.

What unfolds
unfolds

site to which you go
site you bear with you

the sanctum
may be an empty space
vacant, evacuated
invisible
but to inner sight

go out, go in
travel far or stay close to home

what you know   is mystery
what you see   is invisible

but

**"WHETHER THE SACRED SITES ARE LARGE OR SMALL,
WHETHER THEY ARE AT THE CENTER OF THE TOWNS,
IN NEIGHBORHOODS, OR IN THE DEEPEST COUNTRYSIDE,
ESTABLISH ORDINANCES WHICH WILL PROTECT THEM ABSOLUTELY
—SO THAT OUR ROOTS
IN THE VISIBLE SURROUNDINGS
CANNOT BE VIOLATED."**

ARCADES

Somewhere: between here and there
"partly inside, partly outside"
somewhere: sheltered along the way
somewhere: a sheltered way

                                        "the public path
                                        to the building
                                        must itself
                                        become a place"

                    bustling or quiet
                    reflecting the nature
                    of the building and the public
                    space around it

                    toward it

                    away from it

Somewhere to meet
somewhere to talk as we
walk toward or away
in that tapestry
of light and dark

                    the low roof
                    slanting gently down
                    the painted beams sustaining
                    the nesting doves
                    and the slender
                    columns flanking
                    the courtyard

                                        (another
                                        screen
                                        another
                                        invented memory)

We walked on into
that narrow street
covered by awnings
spaced occasionally
so that along
the way shafts of sunlight
broke in

                        the public extended
                        ambiguously into
                        private lives ever
                        so gently so
                        discretely through

        "many doors and windows and half-open walls"

CASCADE OF ROOFS/
SHELTERING ROOF/
ROOF GARDEN

"Seen from afar
the roof of the building
must be made to form
a massive part of the building.

When you see the building, you see the roof."

Whether one comes
seeking protection
seeking opportunity
wealth, romance

One sees the roofs
as a system
One sees the lives they shelter
as a system

"a stable self-buttressing system
which is congruent with
the hierarchy of social spaces
underneath the roofs."

"And a sheltering roof must be placed
so that one can touch it—touch it
from the outside."

Sloping down
along the arcade
sloping down
to the flat roof garden
"terraced for planting
with places to sit and sleep,

private places."

I remember
the sound of rain
on the roof just above
my head

In the room just below
I felt
surrounded
secure

                Or to walk through
                the French doors onto
                the sunlit balcony
                to greet the day

Do you remember the light
seen among the plants
in the pots and window boxes?

Do you remember
the light cascading
upon the great cascade
of roofs, the palaces
and temples, domes and
vaults, the galleries
and theaters, halls of public
assembly when we
approached that city

from afar?

COMMON AREAS AT THE HEART/
COMMUNAL EATING/
FARMHOUSE KITCHEN

We had come seeking something
among *the pans above the stove,*
the pots on the table
We were ghosts but still
fully present in our hunger

> "to say hello to the others
> kiss them, shake hands with them,
> exchange news"   "centered
> around a big table in the middle"

> Our hunger

> passing

through common objects
groups of people
"the informal groups
they want to belong to
in the cities they inhabit"

> "The process hinges entirely
> on the *overlap* of the human groups
> in society, and the way a person
> can pass through these human groups,
>
> expanding his associations"

We remember
because now we are nothing
but the memory—

convivium

—something now lost

"at the center of gravity
of the building complex"

"here they ate, talked,
played cards, and did work of all kinds"

>Families disperse
>and reconstitute themselves
>
>To be alone
>but not to be isolated
>
>Alcoves to the side
>but a single light above the table

CONNECTION TO THE EARTH/SECRET PLACE

Go find a hole
and sit in it
she would say
Not often—
from all reports
I was an easy child
always with his nose
in a book

> *Go find a hole...*
> as if I could run
> down three flights,
> cross the street,
> dodge the cars and buses
> and wander
> into some field!
>
> But now I read that
> "there is continuity. Here,
> there is an intermediate area,
> whose surface is connected
> to the inside of the house"

Was I
deprived?

> "it is as if the earth itself
> becomes in that small area
> a part of your indoor terrain"

> > But in Monroe the porch steps
> > led to worn concrete,
> > slate stepping stones and
> > then the lawn and
> > the spruces I loved

What
they were able to give

Cupboards, open shelves, wardrobes,
cabinets under the stairs, figurines,
bottles of colored glass, old books
waiting to be found in a drawer

Deeper still—"a place
which is virtually impossible to discover"
"a place where the archives of the house,
or other more potent secrets,
might be kept"

Go find a hole…
for what you bring
from the outside gradually
is made part of the inside
the deepest places
the deepest secrets

the clay pot on the dresser
the iron frog rescued
from the garden when
the house was sold
Inscrutable miniatures,
an iconography hidden
but in plain view.

"let the site tell you its secrets"

I began writing poems based on Christopher Alexander's *A Pattern Language* in the fall of 1993, after studying the work for some time. The understanding of form and the idea of community that Alexander and his associates offer in that book moved me and challenged me, and I felt an immediate affinity with the shapes and rhythms of Alexander's sentences, so deliberately expressive of his architectural and decorative vision. As I read my way through the patterns and began writing lyrics based on a few of them—not in the order they are presented, but not randomly either—I gradually realized that I was fulfilling the book's intention in regard to the creation of a given architectural project: that is, a selection of patterns, one of an infinite number of possible sequences, comes together to create a whole. But rather than a building or a park or a neighborhood, my project was a poem.

The sequence was originally called "A Pattern Language" after the book, and I thought that it would be interspersed with the first movements of *Track*, which were written around the same time. But *Track* took on a life of its own, and occupied me for many years. The pattern poems were left behind, though the compelling power of Alexander's work, so practical in application and yet so utopian in scope, remained an important model and source of inspiration for me.

In the summer of 2003, having completed *Powers*, the third and final volume of *Track*, I returned to *A Pattern Language*. The poems from ten years before became section I of the sequence, and I began to write more. Gradually the network expanded into the four-section sequence presented here, which was completed in January, 2005.

About the Author

 **Norman Finkelstein** was born in New York City in 1954. He received his B.A. from Binghamton University and his Ph.D. from Emory University. He is a Professor of English at Xavier University in Cincinnati, Ohio, where he has lived since 1980. His books of poetry include *Restless Messengers* (Georgia, 1992), *Passing Over* (Marsh Hawk, 2007), and the three-volume serial poem *Track: Track* (Spuyten Duyvil, 1999), *Columns* (Spuyten Duyvil, 2002), and *Powers* (Spuyten Duyvil, 2005). He has also written extensively about modern and postmodern poetry, and about Jewish literature. His books of criticism include *Not One of Them In Place: Modern Poetry and Jewish American Identity* (SUNY, 2002) and *Lyrical Interference: Essays on Poetics* (Spuyten Duyvil, 2004). *On Mt. Vision: Forms of the Sacred in Contemporary American Poetry* will be published by the University of Iowa Press in 2010.

Other Poetry Books by Dos Madres Press

Paul Bray - Terrible Woods
Michael Heller - Earth and Cave
Keith Holyoak - My Minotaur
Robert Murphy - Life in the Ordovician
Henry Weinfield - Without Mythologies

* * *

Michael Autrey - From The Genre Of Silence
Paul Bray - Things Past and Things to Come
Jon Curley - New Shadows
Deborah Diemont - The Wanderer
Joseph Donahue - The Copper Scroll
Annie Finch - Home Birth
Norman Finkelstein - An Assembly
Gerry Grubbs - Still Life
Richard Hague - Burst, Poems Quickly
Pauletta Hansel - First Person
Michael Heller - A Look at the Door with the Hinges Off
Michael Henson - The Tao of Longing
Eric Hoffman - Life At Braintree
James Hogan - Rue St. Jaques
Burt Kimmelman - There Are Words
Off The Map - Richard Luftig
J. Morris - The Musician Approaching Sleep
Robert Murphy - Not For You Alone
Peter O'Leary - A Mystical Theology of the Limbic Fissure
David A. Petreman - Luz de Vela en Quintero
David A. Petreman - Candlelight in Quintero
David Schloss - Behind the Eyes
Murray Shugars - Songs My Mother Never Taught Me
Nathan Swartzendruber - Opaque Projectionist
Jean Syed - Sonnets
Henry Weinfield - The Tears of the Muses
Tyrone William - Futures, Elections

www.dosmadres.com